CAPPADOCIA

M E R T
BASIM YAYINCILIK DAĞITIM
VE REKLAMCILIK TİC. LTD. ŞTİ.

CAPPADOCIA

Published and Distributed by
**MERT Basım Yayıncılık Dağıtım
ve Reklamcılık. Tic. Ltd. Şti.**

Text :
Mehmet Çuhadar

Translation :
Dr. Dara Çolakoğlu

Photographs :
Erdal Yazıcı, Güngör Özsoy,
Halûk Özözlü, Tahsin Aydoğmuş,
Şemsi Güner, Firdevs Sayılan

Layout :
Kemal Özdemir

Colour Separation :
Çali Grafik Matbaacılık A.Ş.

ISBN 975-285-101-0

MERT
Basım Yayıncılık Dağıtım
ve Reklamcılık Tic. Ltd. Şti.

İstoç Toptancılar Çarşısı 18.Ada No:51
Mahmutbey, İstanbul - TÜRKİYE
Tel: (0212) 659 68 68-66
Fax: (0212) 659 68 67

2003

FOREWORD

The territory between the central Anatolian cities of Aksaray, Niğde, Nevşehir and Kayseri is historically called Cappadocia, and its unique geological formations and historical heritage startle all visitors who happen to pay a visit. The rocky formations of this territory which have come to existence after mother nature's millions of years of work, and man's contribution to this volcanic area offer to us the breath-taking harmony of man and nature.

Cappadocia harbors an infinite number of tumuli and antique cities because it has been home to the most various peoples since time began. All of these treasures are still waiting to be discovered by archaeologists who can contribute a great deal to the history of this region. Two of these antique cities which have been excavated till now and have illuminated Anatolian history to a certain extent are Kültepe near Kayseri, and Acemhöyük in Aksaray's vicinity.

Cappadocia is simultaneously the area where one of the greatest civilizations of Anatolia, that of the Hittites, was founded and had flourished. It is therefore full with the beautiful traces of that antique civilization. Among the Hittite reliefs of the region we see those of Emirgazi, İmamkulu, Fraktin, Andaval, Göllüdağ, and Bor. Furthermore we have the Sivas, Sultanhanı, Andaval, and Karapınar inscriptions and a number of Hittite cities as remnants of this past glory.

After the fall of the Hittite Empire, Cappadocia came to be called the Tabal Land which was then ruled by the Phyrigians, Lydians, Persians, Macedonians and the Ariarathes Dynasty one after the other. Its military significance grew in the Roman Period and during the early Christian era, it witnessed an immense population growth. Thousands of churches and monasteries were built in this area according to the necessities of the monastic life, the rules of which the clergyman Basilius, a native of Cappadocia, had determined in the 4th century A.D. The natives of Cappadocia were always confronted with raids coming from the east and the south in the Byzantine era. They therefore had to construct their monasteries away from the main roads and in hidden valleys. The invading Persians coming from the east and the Arabs streaming in from the south devastated this region starting with the 7th century A.D. The local population of the times built the underground cities of the volcanic rocks which are now called " the eighth wonder of the world", and sought refuge in them. In the same period, the Iconoclastic Crisis broke out in the Byzantine Empire which had the impression of being a movement against painting and imagery, but was actually a political maneuver to subdue the power of the church. The Iconoclastic Crisis got hold of the region of Cappadocia as well. When the Arab invasions and the conoclastic Crisis were over, hundreds of new churches were built in Cappadocia, and they were decorated with the most beautiful paintings and ornaments possible. Priest Jerphanion, who has made the most painstaking research in this area, called the churches of that period, " the archaic churches", and stated that they were very freely decorated with pictures as a reaction to the Iconoclastic Period preceding it. Cappadocia witnessed the construction of the biggest and grandiose churches in the 10th century A.D indeed, but the golden age of the region took place in the following century. Especially the churches in and around Göreme are outstanding in architectural planning and iconographical creativity. But the 11th century A.D was also a time of great wars and political tumult. The Seldjuk Turks who immigrated to Asia Minor in this period fought hard against the Crusaders, who had set out from Europe to banish the Byzantine Empire and the Turks from Anatolia, and reach the Holy Land. The Seldjuk Turks erected unsurpassed examples of religious, military and

Natural formations near Uçhisar.

civilian buildings in this period and in the 13th century which is termed to be the golden age of the Seldjuk Empire. That the names of the Seldjuk Sultan Mesud and the Byzantine Emperor Andronicus are mentioned together in the church of St. Georgius in the valley of Ihlara, is a good indicator of the Seldjuk tolerance towards the Christian population which built their churches and practiced their religion freely. We see the Seldjuk monuments mainly in Aksaray, Niğde, Nevşehir, and Kayseri which were on the caravan roads reaching Cappadocia. After the Seldjuk Empire was defeated by the Mongols in the 13th century, a number of principalities were formed all over Anatolia. The smallest of these principalities which was geographically closest to Byzantine Constantinople, namely the Ottomans, emerged as the strongest state and grew rapidly to form

Typical scenes from the roads leading to Cappadocia.

The famous dolls of Cappadocia.

Folkdance group at a performance.

The living-room of a typical village house near Ürgüp.

an empire extending to Europe, Asia, and African shores. The chief Ottoman monuments of Anatolia are seen mostly in Kayseri, Ürgüp, Niğde, Avanos, and Nevşehir. Particularly Nevşehir, which was the home town of the Grand Visier Damat İbrahim Pasha of the Tulip Era, was filled with numerous religious and civil buildings.

The churches of Cappadocia were belittled as " works of provincial art" for a long time, but they show us all the consecutive stages of Byzantine art. Since they were erected throughout the Byzantine era, they display Byzantine architecture, iconography, and the art of painting from the beginning till its end. The research done in these churches show us clearly that the wall paintings have been done by the same artists and indeed by certain schools of painters. This fact and the existence of churches

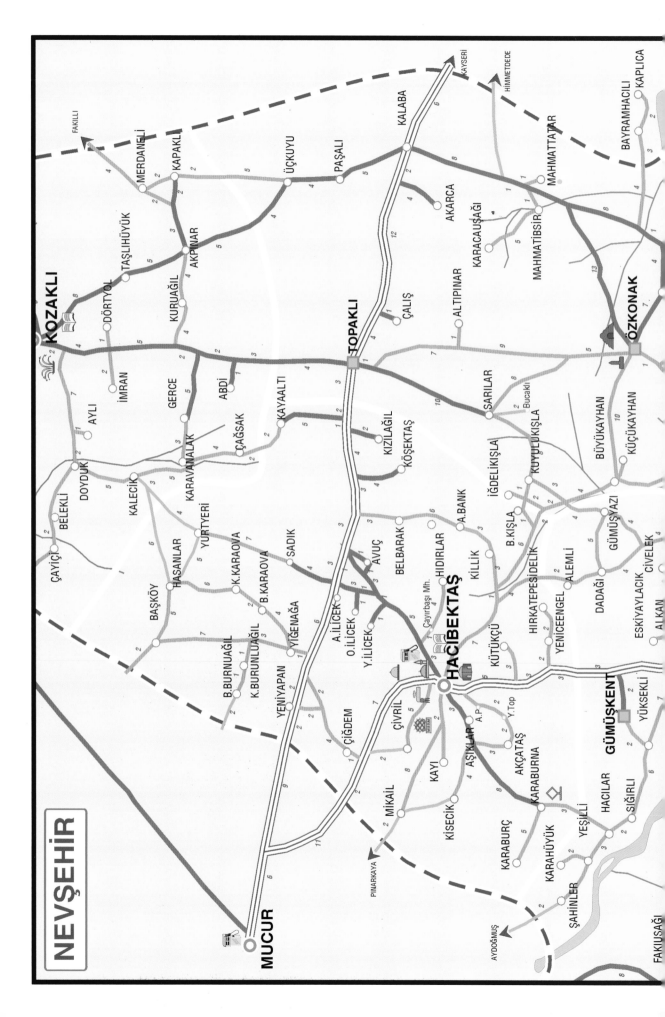

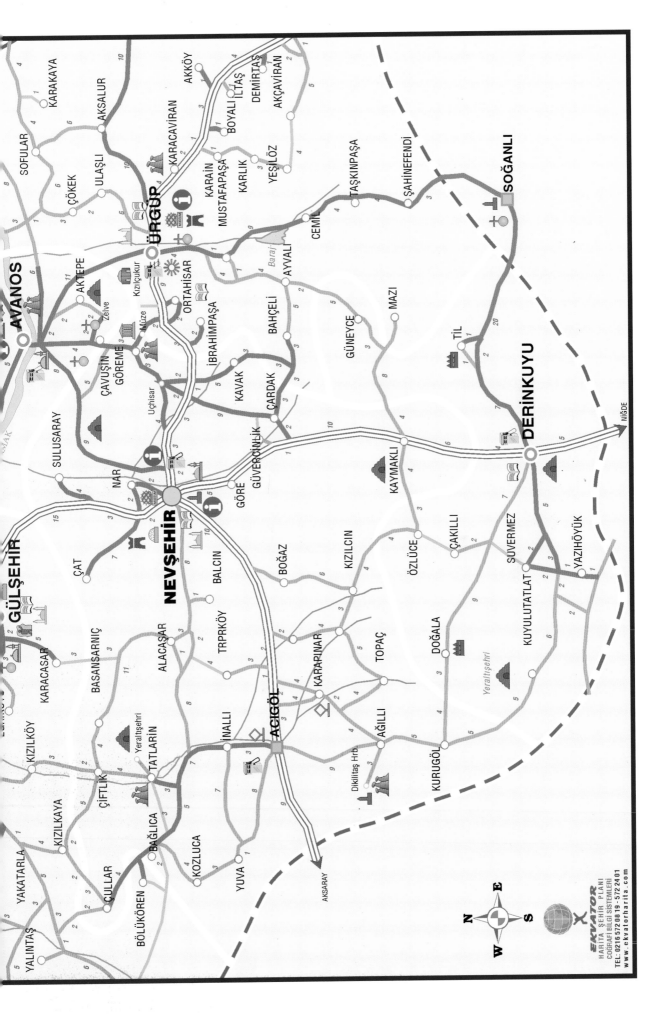

that were dedicated to emperors and to the clergy indicate that the local churches have not been the works of religious leaders and local artists only. Especially the churches of the Ihlara valley show Egyptian and Palestinian influences that were moulded in Cappadocia to form local interpretations. To analyze the artistic importance of these churches is surely one side of the coin, but the thousands of pictures seen on the church walls deliver crucial clues to the beliefs and the traditions of the times, and illuminate the secrets of the monastic life of the region.

The recent years have shown that we should preserve the natural wonders of Cappadocia and its immense cultural heritage to a much wider extent. Nature herself which is the sole creator of this incredible beauty also destroys the cultural residue as she goes on creating new formations. Rock settlements collapse because of erosion and the local population deserts the erosion of not having a direct influence over the natural and cultural history of the region. They must, therefore, be placed under the strictest control possible. The hotels between Nevşehir and Uçhisar which is

the most renowned symbol of Cappadocia per se, and the buildings we see when we look at Ortahisar from the hills of Göreme overshadow the unmatched view of Cappadocia and Erciyes. The mistakes which are being made for the sake of tourism should never be pardoned, and the territory between Aksaray, Nevşehir, and Kayseri must be respected and protected with all our might.

Two typical views from Cappadocia.

11

CAPPADOCIA

The geological formation of Cappadocia is a natural wonder of our world and is the result of two contradicting natural forces. One of these forces is the volcanic outspurts of the region which led to its coverage with lava, ashes, tuff, and volcanic residue. The second force then is the territorial erosion that started after the volcanic build up was over.

The Taurus Mountains of south Anatolia emerged at the Tertiary stage of the geological development just like the European Alps have been (65- 2 million years prior to our time). In this stage of

"mountain building", deep crevasses and subsidences occurred in central Anatolia. The molten rock (magma) at the earth's core emerged to the surface through these crevasses and formed the volcanoes of Erciyes, Develi, Melendiz and Keçiboyduran. These volcanoes formed a volcano chain parallel to the Taurus mountains and strong erruptions followed. The volcanic lava, ashes and tuff moved slowly towards the subsidences of the region and covered the formerly shaped hills and valleys, thus turning the whole region into the huge plateau we see now.

The reasons of the erosion which rendered Cappadocia its present scenery

Natural wonders near Göreme.

12

The famous fairy chimneys of Ürgüp.

have been the winds, the rivers, and the rains. The other factors of the scenic formation of Cappadocia are the climate of the region with its sharp temperature changes, and the melting snow of the mountains. These sharp changes in temperature gave way to splits in the rocks which were filled up with rain water. As these crevasses froze in winter, the rocks cracked and seperated, but the main factors of erosion have been the rains and the rivers.The Nevşehir and Damsa streams which flow into the Kızılırmak river played the major role in the formation of the famous cappadocian valleys. Particularly the area between Nevşehir, Avanos, and Ürgüp, where the

thickness of the tuffs in the old valleys reached almost a hundred meters, got extremely affected by erosions. The rain waters filled up the crevasses on the surface of the plateau and gave birth to the streams and rivers. The volcanic residues and the eroded earth got carried away by the rivers which sometimes cut the volcanic surface so sharply, that seperate hills came into existence.

THE FAIRY CHIMNEYS

The fairy chimneys which render a fabulous scenery to Cappadocia are the results of a geological phenomenon that lasted for millions of years. The story of the fairy chimneys which are unique in the world starts with the volcanic eruptions of this region.

We come across the most beautiful fairy chimneys in the area which is 288 square kilometers big and lies between an 18 kilometer section of Kızılırmak in the north, the Damsa stream in the east, the Nevşehir stream in the west, and the Oylu and Kermil mountains in the south. This volcanic area is built by the tuffs underneath, and basalt and andesites over them. The latter covered the tuffs wholly once, but today they are seen only in some sections. These basalt pieces stand either as huge blocks on the conical shapes, or as cornices over the tuffs. The fairy chimneys came into existence at the suitable areas through the rains and the erosions of the 4th Geologic Time. They sometimes reach a height of 40 meters, are conical in shape, and have a " hat" of basalt over them. The phenomenon of erosion thins out the neck underneath the " hat" which in the end can't be carried by the cone anymore and drops down. Such a fairy chimney will then be left without protection and will be eroded further. This phenomenon takes place continually even today and the very old chimneys get replaced by the younger ones. We find the best examples of these natural wonders in the triangle between Ürgüp, Uçhisar, and Avanos.

The fairy chimneys are the symbols of Cappadocia.

s.16-17: More fairy chimneys from Cappadocia.

E R C İ Y E S

Erciyes is one of the highest mountains (3917 m) of Anatolia and is situated at the south-west of Kayseri. It's the foremost volcanic mountain of the region whose volcanic activity started in the miocenic stage and lasted until the recent geologic time.

The Erciyes Mountain has a diameter of 18 kilometers and covers an area of 1500 square meters, with volcanic basins to its east that reach up to heights of 1200-1700 meters. Erciyes which looks older and shabbier than the Hasandağ, spurted out tuffs and then andesites during its volcanic activity. Towards the end stage of this active period it also erupted basalt lava.

The peak of this volcanic mountain which the Hittites called " Harkassos" or " the White Mountain" is always covered with snow. The Hittite Pantheon which comprised almost a thousand gods, also had very significant mountain gods, one of which is believed to be the Erciyes Mountain.

The mountain gods of the Hittites are seen clearly on the reliefs we know today. The ancient peoples have worshipped Erciyes for long ages and this mountain god emerges as an important deity even at the Roman period, together with the emperor and jupiter cults. Erciyes which was then called " Argieus", appears on all the minted coins of this region.

Kayseri, the Erciyes Mountain.

A superb view of Hasandağı.

HASANDAĞI

Hasandağ is one of the most beautiful mountains of Anatolia, and is 2300 meters higher than the plateau at its foot and 3300 meters above sea level. This double-peaked mountain has come to existence in the same period as the Erciyes but looks much younger. It welcomes the guests of Cappadocia in all its splendor and is covered with snow almost throughout the year.

THE RIVER OF MELENDİZ

The Melendiz river is born at the foot of the Melendiz Mountain and is one of the crucial rivers of the Cappadocia region. Melendiz is fed by quite a number of streams, and as it passes through Ihlara and the Selime village, it creates the famous Ihlara Canyon.

KIZILIRMAK (The Red River)

Kızılırmak is the longest river of Turkey. It's born in the east of the country and draws a big loop in central Anatolia before it rises northwards and flows into the Black Sea. Kızılırmak is approximately 1182 kilometers long and it's named after the color of its waters. This river and its streams are one of the sources of Cappadocia's wonderful scenery. The Hittites called it "Marassantia" and in the Graeco-Roman period its name was "Hallys". The loop of this river is, along with other civilizations, the cradle of the Hittite Empire.

19

THE HISTORY OF CAPPADOCIA

THE FRESCO OF ÇATALHÖYÜK

We can accept that the long history of Cappadocia starts with a wall fresco found in the oldest neolithic city of Çatalhöyük. This wall fresco is renowned as the oldest scenic painting of the world and shows one of the volcanic mountains of the region, namely the Hasandağ. On this fresco which is dated back to 6200 B.C, we see the houses of Çatalhöyük in the front with the mountain's smoke, volcanic bombs, and the flowing lava as its setting. This fresco with the double-peaked Hasandağ is now at the Museum of Anatolian Civilizations in Ankara. The fresco is an indicator of the decorative taste of the local population of those times. It is furthermore geologically important in that, it is a proof of the volcanic activity of Hasandağ which was eternally carved on a plate by a local artist.

Cappadocia witnessed the existence of a series of small and independent kingdoms ruled by princes in 5000-4000 B.C. The most important city of this period has been " Pruskanda".

This is also the period when the Anatolian peoples took up commercial relations with their eastern, northern, and southern neighbors. These relations have not always been free of friction, and we see that 17 Anatolian kings (including the king of Cappadocia- Kanesh) have united in 2300 B.C against the Assyrian king Naramsin, and that this block has fought with him. This union is also the very first alliance of Anatolian history ever mentioned.

THE AGE OF ASSYRIAN TRADE COLONIES

Anatolia entered her golden age at the beginning of 2000 B.C and became the

Kültepe, the Kanesh trade colony.

Natural formations near Uçhisar.

most attractive place for immigrants. The Assyrians, who were well-known for their commercial cunning, were of course aware of the riches of this peninsula, and have founded " Karum"s, that is trade centers, in the most promising localities of Anatolia. The leading Karum of the times was the one founded in Kültepe. The Karum of Kültepe was situated at the outskirts of the castle of Kanish. The Assyrians imported tin, textiles, perfumes and other luxury articles to Anatolia, and exported gold, silver and copper in return. This queer trade between the Assyrian merchants and the locals of Anatolia lasted as long as 150 years. The wars among the Anatolian kingdoms in 1850-1800 B.C put an end to the age of the Assyrian trade colonies.

This era has attracted the attention of many researchers and archaeologists since the beginning of the 19th century, and finally an Assyrian trade colony was excavated in Kültepe/ Cappadocia in 1925. One of the main discoveries of this excavation was the " Tablets of Cappadocia" which are the oldest written documents of Anatolian history, and which are therefore of immesurable importance.

THE HITTITES

The tribes which settled in Anatolia at the beginning of the 2nd millenium B. C are called the Hittites. They got integrated into the highly developed civilization of the Hatti, the original inhabitants of Anatolia. The migration routes of the Hittites are still disputable but they are generally accepted to have come down to Anatolia over Caucassus. The early clay tablets of the Hittites mention a number of kings, the most important of whom has been Anitta, who had chosen Kültepe to build his capital. The Hittites

21

founded their empire in Cappadocia but expanded it to such an extent, that they conquered Aleppo and Babylonia, and overthrew the Hammurabi Dynasty of Babylonia. As a result of their expansion, they established close ties with the local peoples of Mesopotamia and Syria.

The strength of the Hittite Empire reached its peak in the 15th and 14th centuries B.C. This was an epoch when the lands of Syria and Palestine turned out to be the battle ground of the wars between the Hittites and the Egyptians. It finally came to an end with the war of Kadesh and the peace treaty following it, which was signed by the Hittite king Hattusilis III and the Egyptian pharaoh Rameses II in 1286 B.C. The Hittite Empire was conquered by the " sea tribes" coming from Europe in the 12th century B.C and a period of social tumult began. One of these warlike tribes was the Phyrigians who founded a state and stopped the political unrest in Anatolia.

THE TABAL LAND

The region of Cappadocia was named "the Tabal land" after the downfall of the Hittite Empire. The inhabitants of this region wanted to have friendly relations with the Assyrian Kingdom but was continually attacked by it throughout the 10th- 7th centuries B.C. This span of time is named the " Dark Age" of Anatolia and Cappadocia.

THE PERSIANS

Cappadocia fell under the sovereignty of the Kingdom of Lydia in the 6th century B.C and remained so until Croesus, the king of Lydia, was defeated by the Persians. As a result, Cappadocia was ruled by the Persians between the 6th century B.C and the arrival of Alexander the Great in Anatolia. The Persians divided Anatolia into provinces each one of which was ruled by a governor, called a "satrap". The

A wiev from dreamland of Paşabağ.

governance of the Persians was mild and tolerant, and they managed to establish friendly relationships with the local population. The main source of revenue of the Persian economy was the famous King's Road which, starting from Ephesos and Sardes, ran through Mazaka (Kayseri) and going over Mesopotamia, reached the Persian capital of Susa. The Satraps used to send gold, sheep, mules, and the famous horses of Cappadocia as tax to Persia. The Persians who were fire worshippers must have liked this volcanic area very much, and have found it suitable for their animistic traditions.

THE HORSES OF CAPPADOCIA

The horses and the stud farms of Cappadocia have been famous throughout history. The tradition of giving horses as tribute is supposed to have originated here, and antique sources mention the horses presented to the Assyrian king Assurbanipal and the Persian kings Darius and Xerxes as gifts. It is also believed that the word Cappadocia comes from the word "Catpaducia", meaning " the land of beautiful horses".

Another kingly visitor of the region was Alexander the Great who came to Cappadocia after he broke up the renowned Gordian knot. But he didn't stay long and moved on after appointing general Cabictas as the ruler of this region.

Cappadocia was then ruled by the Macedonians until the death of Alexander the Great. The Ariarathes Dynasty took over thereafter and founded the independent kingdom of Cappadocia with Eusebeia i.e Kayseri of today, as their capital. The subjects of this kingdom sought to establish peace with the subjects of the other Anatolian kingdoms through marriages. But such alliances lead involuntarily to political and interfamilial struggles among the

Two typical views from Cappadocia.

kingdoms of Pontus, Bythinia, and the Roman Empire. The rule of the Ariarathes Dynasty lasted until 90 B.C when Mithridates, the King of Pontus, appointed his son to the throne of the Cappadocian Kingdom. Cappadocia fell under Roman rule in 66 B.C, but the political tumult in the region lasted until 17 A.D when Cappadocia became a province of the Pax Romana. Cappadocia is one of the most sterile areas of Anatolia with regard to Greek and Roman inscriptions. We have only a few epitaphs left over.

THE ROMAN ERA

In the era of the Roman emperor Vespasianus, two Roman legions have been stationed in Cappadocia in order to protect it against a probable Parthian invasion coming from the east. The Romans also built military routes here in the time of emperor Trajan. The Roman emperor Hadrian was also interested in the region and visited Cappadocia in 129 A.D entering Anatolia from its eastern borders. In the 3rd century A.D the commercial relations between Cappadocia, Ephesos, and Smyrna grew to be very intense, and coins were minted bearing the names of these places together. We also know that the cities on this main trade route got together to form an economic union.

THE BYZANTINE ERA

Three religious leaders have played an important role in the history of Cappadocia during the 4th century A.D. These are Basilius the Great, Gregorius of Nyssa, and Gregorius of Naziansus who have set up the principles of monastic life in this region. Basilius the Great, who descended from a wealthy family of Kayseri (Caesaria), visited the monasteries of Palestine and Egypt first and investigated the then existing principles of monastic life there. He saw that asceticism and contemplative abstraction were being practiced to achieve spiritual perfection. Basilius did not accept these practices and determined some newer principles: He stood up for a monastic life where monks would live in small groups and be submissive to the orders of their superiors, hoping to prevent their abstraction from social life. He wanted the monks to indulge in social life, and help the ill and the needy, instead of following an abstinence that would resemble the monastic life in Palestine and Egypt. The first city where his theories were put to practice was the city of Basiliad, founded by himself in the vicinity of Kayseri. Basilius held his principles to be the most effective defence mechanisms against laziness which supposedly destroyed the inner equilibrium of the monks. The monks adopted these ideas and built hundreds of monasteries in the following ages becoming, thus, involved in public life instead of leading an abstract life like the monks of the Athos and the Meteora monasteries in Greece.

The first decorated churches of this region were built in the 6th and 7th centuries A.D. Especially the 7th century was the time of Persian and Arab invasions consecutively, and the most important city of Cappadocia, Kayseri, could not resist these raids and was captured by the invading powers quite a number of times. This threat forced the Byzantine state and the inhabitants to take precautions against possible invasions. They built numerous fortresses upon the roads leading to Cappadocia from the south, and developed a "light signaling system" which would enable the news of the enemy reach Cappadocia and Constantinople and spread like wild-fire. This system which we can call a "light telegraph", rendered the news of a threat from the south reach Constantinople within an hour. The Byzantine army was seperated into independent " themes" which could draw their own strategies and fight accordingly. The last link of this chain of protection and defence was the underground cities,

An unmatched view from the valley of Göreme.

where thousands of inhabitants could seek refuge and hide in for a long period.

The Byzantine empire went through the Iconoclastic Crisis between 726-843 A.D when figurative painting was prohibited and banned.

Cappadocia was visited by the famous emperor Nicephorus Phocas and his family in 964-965 A.D. This emperor who was a native of Cappadocia himself, was one of the best commanders of the Byzantine army and won consecutive glories in the wars against the invading Arabs. He had married empress Theophano upon the death of her spouse, emperor Romanus II, and had acquired the crown. Though he was a great soldier, the emperor was also interested in monastic life, and the Church of Çavuşin was built in his honor.

THE SELDJUK PERIOD

The nomadic Turks streamed into Anatolia starting with the 9th century A.D. The war of Manzikert (1071) which took place between the Seldjuk Turks and the Byzantine army is accepted to be the final defeat of the Byzantinians and the last obstacle for the Turks to get hold of the peninsula.

The following centuries witnessed great wars between the Seldjuk Turks, the Byzantine empire, and the Crusaders. The Seldjuk Turks who lost their first capital İznik (Nicea) during one of the crusades, moved their capital to Konya (Ikonium) in central Anatolia.

The Seldjuk empire was the first state founded by Turks on Anatolian soil. The Seldjuk empire which had a relatively short life but startles us with fabulous political, military, commercial, and architectural success and monuments, paved the way to the following Ottoman empire.

The Seldjuks had conquered Kayseri in 1082 and built a number of monuments also in Cappadocia.

The most significant of these are the Grand Mosque of Kayseri (1135-1150), the Alaeddin Mosque in Aksaray (1156), the Double Medrese (school) in Kayseri (1202), the Kayseri School of Medicine (1206), the Alaeddin Mosque in Niğde (1206), the Sahibiye Medrese in Kayseri (1268), and the Sungur Bey Mosque in Niğde (1268).

But the most outstanding monuments of the Seldjuk period are undoubtedly the caravanserais.

The Seldjuk Turks who established commercial relations with other Islamic countries and conquered Sinope (1204) at the Black Sea coast and Attalia (1207) at the Meditteranean, sought to expand the volume of trade and to guarantee the security and comfort of the travellers. This outlook led to the construction of the caravanserais of immense artistic importance.

The number of caravanserais built upon the road between Konya and Kayseri reached 20.

The Seldjuk Turks for whom trade was of extreme significance, offered travellers food, shelter and medical services since the reign of Sultan Kılıçarslan II. The mosques, baths, hospitals, and stud farms of these caravanserais show clearly that these monuments were not only meant for travellers.

They were usually built 30-40 kilometers away from each other, and were fortified with high walls and watch towers for military purposes. They offered comfort and security at times of peace, but at war they were the headquarters of the empire's military personnel.

Typical scenes from the road leading to Cappadocia.

THE SULTANHANI

The Sultanhanı on the road between Aksaray and Konya was built by the Seldjuk Sultan Alaeddin Keykubad in 1229. It is one of the most outstanding examples of Turkish art on Anatolian soil and covers an area of 4500 square meters.

This "han" is composed of a winter and a summer section, and resembles a real fortress with its unending walls and watch towers.

Even the name of the chief construction worker, Muhammed bin Çavlan, is mentioned on a medallion of the inscript at the portal. Through the very ornate portal of the caravanserai we enter the inner courtyard where we see the rooms, the bath, and the storerooms lined one after the other. Right in the middle of the courtyard there is a small mosque (mescit) which rests upon a high tower.

A second portal leads us to the covered section of the caravanserai which is divided into five esplanades. Over the middle esplanade which is higher than the rest, we see a dome that lets more daylight enter the place.

Sultanhanı, a general view.

Sultanhanı, the monumental portal.

THE VALLEY OF
I H L A R A

The breath-taking natural beauty of the Ihlara valley has formed at the outskirts of the volcanic Hasandağ. The outpouring of this double-peaked volcano and of the Göllüdağ near it covered the terrain with layers of tuff and lava. The Melendiz river then cut through these 100 meter thick layers creating a canyon which is 15 kilometers long and 150 meters deep. The fairy chimneys in the Selime and Yaprakhisar villages of this region are of outstanding beauty. The valley of Ihlara does not only surprise the visitors with its natural beauty, but possesses a unique historical heritage as well. The valley of Ihlara which lies between the Ihlara village and the Selime village to its north, is actually eight kilometers long with bird's flight, but

because the valley draws almost 30 meanders between these villages, the road extends to 15 kilometers for the visitor.

We get the best information over the early history of the Hasandağ region from two excavations done there. One of these is the excavation of Aşıklı Hüyük near Aksaray, where the finds of the neolithic and the calcolithic periods and the obsidian pieces discovered, inform us on the geological history of this ancient city. The second excavation is the one done in Acem Höyük also near Aksaray. Acem Höyük has been one of the biggest settlements of ancient Anatolia where the calcolithic, Assyrian Trade Colonies, Hittite, Hellenistic, and Roman layers rendered crucial information on the Hasandağ region.

Aksaray and the area around it were situated on the main commercial routes, and this region was continually attacked

after the 7th century A.D. We have stated that the Byzantine empire and the local inhabitants took measures against these attacks coming from the south. Just as they built fortresses along the roads leading to this area from the south, they developed a "light signaling system" which enabled the news of the coming enemy reach Cappadocia and Constantinople within an hour. The Byzantine army was also divided into independent and mobile divisions called "Themes".

The early Christians built a number of monasteries in the valleys of Ihlara and Belisırma. These valleys were almost hidden from the eye and were geographically hard to reach, therefore they didn't suffer so much from the invading strangers of the 7th century A.D. The churches built by the inhabitants in the 7th- 13th centuries are an evidence for this lucky escape. After the Seldjuk

Turks came to this area and founded their empire, the names of the Seldjuk Sultan and the Byzantine emperor appeared together in one of the churches. In our opinion, this situation is to be interpreted as an evidence of the seldjuk tolerance towards the Christian population.

The valleys of Ihlara and Belisırma have been a place of flight for many monks coming from Egypt, Palestine and Syria.

This is one of the reasons why we can witness the foreign influences on the paintings, architecture and iconography of the area. It was not until recent times that these hidden valleys attracted the attention of researchers and historians. The French researchers Nicole and Michel Thierry started to observe and investigate Cappadocia in 1950, and with the consistent publications of the Ihlara specialists since 1958, visitors from all

over the world started to flow to this region.

THE CHURCH OF AĞAÇALTI

One of the oldest churches of Cappadocia is the St. Daniel's Church and it dates back to the 6th century A.D. Its groundplan is in the shape of a cross and the central cupola has the painting of the Resurrection. This church is named after the figures of St. Daniel and of a lion at the western wall which have been partly preserved. The other important biblical scenes seen in this church are that of the Annunciation, the visit, the flight from Egypt, and the Epiphany.

THE CHURCH OF PÜRENLİ SEKİ

This church is very small and has a single hall. It dates back to the 10th century A.D. At the narthex we see the scenes of the 40 saints of Sebasta, the last judgment, and the Deisis. Inside the church we find the scenes of Annunciation, Maria's visit to Elizabeth, the birth of Jesus, the Epiphany, and Jesus turns water to wine.

THE SERPENT CHURCH

The pictures of the Serpent Church display Egyptian and Syrian influences, and the colors and the iconography in this church stand wide apart from those of the other churches.

The crucial scene at the entrance show the women being attacked by the snakes and their sins are written beside them. This picture shows that women who are quilty of adultery, forgery, disobedience, and of abstinence from breast-feeding are to be attacked by horrible snakes.

THE CHURCH OF EĞRİTAŞ

This church is at the other side of the river and is almost in ruins. It has been

built at the end of the 9th century A.D. A number of tombstones in and around the church show that it is one of the oldest monastic churches of this region. There's a huge cross painted inside the dome. In the church of Egritaş we see such scenes as the Annunciation, the Epiphany, the washing of the feet, and St. Petrus' denial of Christ.

THE VALLEY OF BELISIRMA

The majority of the churches in this valley, which is not often visited, have been built in the Byzantine tradition. The churches of Sümbüllü and Direkli, and the Ala Church are outstanding examples of the Byzantine architecture of the 10th and 11th centuries. Especially the church of Direkli with its beautiful wall- painting is a reminder of the golden age which started after the era of Arabic invasions. The St. George Church which is also in the valley of Belisırma dates back to 1295, and shows the names of the Seldjuk Sultan Mesud and of the Byzantine Emperor Andronicus written together. This situation is proof enough for the religious freedom the Christian inhabitants of the times enjoyed under Seldjuk rule.

A typical view from the village of Belisırma

Güzelyurt, one of the houses famous for stone-carving.

Güzelyurt, a general view.

GÜZELYURT

Güzelyurt which was called Gelveri in antiquity is an important settlement that is situated at the slope of a hill 12 kilometers to the west of the Ihlara valley.

Güzelyurt's beautifully painted stone houses, differently planned churches, and edifices carved out of rocks surprise every visitor to the utmost.

The catchiest of the churches here is the one which was dedicated to Gregory of Naziansus, and which has been turned into a mosque today. It has a cross plan, a high tambour with a cupola, and is constructed with squared stones.

The Christian communities which lived here under Seldjuk and Ottoman rules left this area after the Treaty of Lausanne (1924) was signed and a Turkish-Greek population exchange was put to practice.

The Monastery Valley which is 4 kilometers away from Güzelyurt harbors innumerable churches and monasteries, showing us that Güzelyurt has once been an important religious center.

AĞZIKARAHAN

Ağzıkarahan is situated not far away from Aksaray and is very well preserved. It was one of the main caravanserais on the road between Konya and Kayseri. The inscription over the monumental portal through which we enter the winter section, tells us that the construction of this caravanserai has been started by master Hodja Mesud bin Abdullah in the reign of the Seldjuk Sultan Alaeddin Keykubad, and was finished under Sultan Gıyaseddin Keyhüsrev.

At the portals of this caravanserai geometric designs replace human and animal figures, and floral decorations. We see a small mosque built on pillars right in the middle of the main courtyard.

ALAYHAN

This caravanserai is on the road between Aksaray and Nevşehir, and was erected by the Seldjuk Sultan Kılıçarslan II in 1192.

Alayhan is only 35 kilometers away from Aksaray, and is of crucial importance because it's the first caravanserai built in the reign of the Seldjuk Turks. Its walls are ruined but the incredibly ornamented portal is still erect in all its splendor.

The stone-masonry of the Seldjuks seen on this portal amazes all art lovers. An interesting detail of this portal is the single-faced and double-torsoed lion figure which is believed to represent Sultan Kılıçarslan II.

Ağzıkarahan, a view of the courtyard.

Ağzıkarahan, the monumental portal.

AĞZIKARAHAN

N E V Ş E H I R

Nevşehir was a little Anatolian town called "Muskara" until the beginning of the 18th century. The fate of the town changed with the life of Damat İbrahim Pasha who was its native. İbrahim Pasha was introduced to the Ottoman court in İstanbul as a confectioner's apprentice but rose rapidly with his diligence, intellect, and cunning. He became advisor to the Ottoman Sultan Ahmed III, and then was appointed pasha and got higher jobs. After getting married to the Sultan's daughter, Fatma Sultan, he was appointed Grand Visier of the state. This art-lover of the Tulip Era of Ottoman history promoted the public improvement of his native town with his own income. First he changed the name of his town to Nevşehir (New City), and enrolled it in the register so that it wouldn't be changed again. He erected mosques, schools, baths, caravanserais, and libraries in this new city and exempted the immigrants from all taxes. The population of Nevşehir soon reached 17 000. İbrahim Pasha distributed the lands of the treasury to the new-comers and established mulberry fields at the outskirts of the city, so that the silk industry would flourish. This public improvement was infringed a little after his death in 1730, but the city's economic importance continued. It became the capital of the Nevşehir province in 1954.

The oldest building of Nevşehir, which is full of religious and civil buildings erected in both the Seldjuk and the Ottoman periods, is the fortress on the highest hill of the city left from the Seldjuk times. This Seldjuk fortress with

Nevşehir, a general view.

double portals was repaired by İbrahim Pasha and fortified by watch towers. The most significant building of the city is the İbrahim Pasha complex consisting of a mosque, a university, a library, a bath, a public kitchen, and a school for elementary education, all built in the 18th century. The mosque of this complex is called the Kurşunlu Cami which has a square plan, and a poem of the famous poet Nedim of the Tulip Era over the portal that leads to the main courtyard. The dome eaves of the fountain in the courtyard and the interior of the mosque are decorated with the rich ornaments of the Tulip Era. Another mosque erected by İbrahim Pasha is the Kaya Camii dating back to 1715 which has a square plan and a very plain style.

Nevşehir, two views of the Kurşunlu Cami.

p.40-41: An illustrated scene showing the daily life in an underground dwelling.

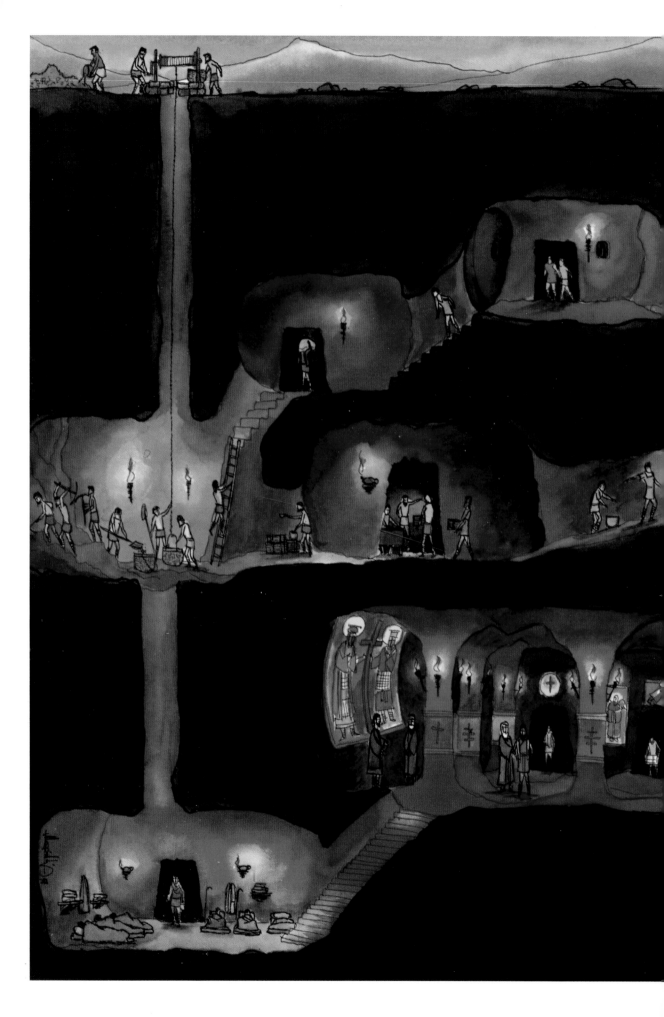

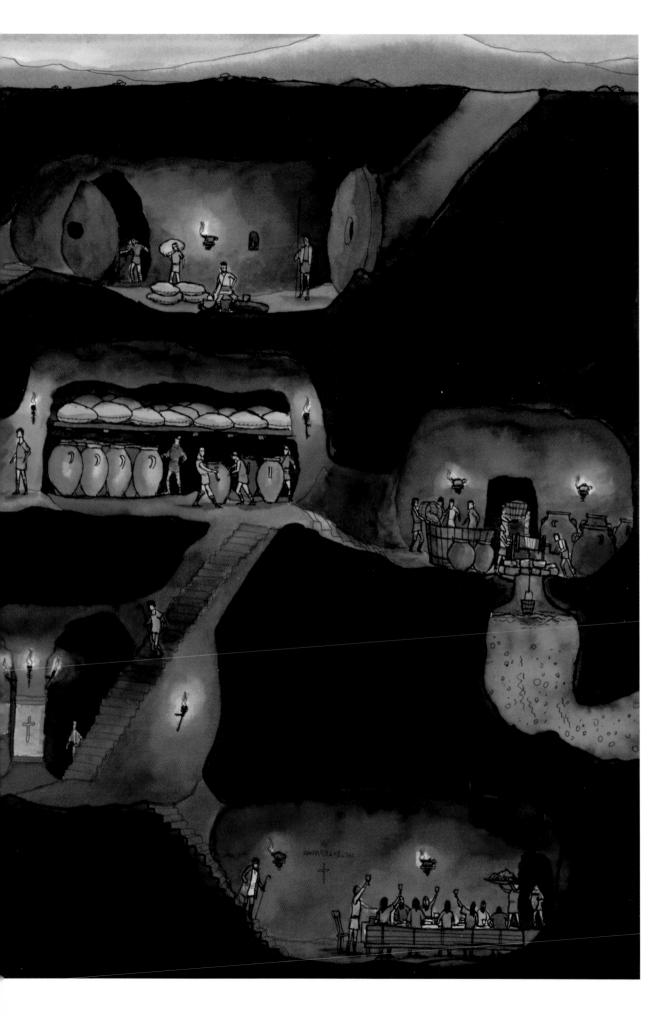

THE UNDERGROUND CITIES

The most amazing speciality of Cappadocia is the underground cities which are still being discovered. Among the countless underground cities of the region, the ones in Kaymaklı and in Derinkuyu are most famous ones. These cities with 8-9 floors which have been completely carved in volcanic tuff, resemble labyrinths with their innumerate rooms, narrow tunnels, and ventilation systems.

Though people settled in these cities before Christianity, they were mainly used during the Arab invasions.

The Arabs never conquered this area but they plundered it, and we know today that the Christian population sought refuge in these underground cities temporarily. The narrow tunnels which could be blocked by millstones at times of escape, the ventilation systems, and the hidden rooms of these cities show a perfect planning and construction.

All the utensils for daily use like tables, chairs, and beds and the living areas like rooms, wine production sections, storerooms, and churches are carved out of rocks.

The ventilation systems of the underground cities are so well-made, that we get fresh air even at the deepest floor. But questions like where the excavated earth has been carried, how long their construction lasted, and who has really lived in these cities are still unanswered. The absence of inscriptions and decorations of any kind makes it difficult for the art historians to determine the dates of construction.

The underground city of Kaymaklı.

KAYMAKLI

Kaymaklı which is situated 20 kilometers to the south of Nevşehir has developed rapidly in recent years and become attractive for tourists. The underground city of Kaymaklı lies underneath the Kaymaklı castle which is to the east of the Kaymaklı village. This underground city is accepted to have been built in the 6th-10th centuries at the time of Persian and Arab invasions, and is accessible since 1964. It spreads over an area of 2,5 square kilometers, and we can estimate that it has 7-8 floors though all of the floors have not been discovered yet. The plan of Kaymaklı differs from that of the underground city of Derinkuyu, in that the tunnels joining the floors are narrower, steeper, and shorter. The living rooms of the four floors which have already been excavated are situated primarily around the ventilation chimneys. There is a rather small stable at

The underground city of Kaymaklı.

the first floor and most probably other ones in the floors we haven't seen yet. The road at the left of this stable leads us to a small church with a single hall and two apsides which is on the second floor. This tiny church has no wall-paintings and therefore we cannot date it. The grave rooms on the second floor are thought to have belonged to the clergy. The most important rooms of this underground city are on the third floor. There are plenty of storerooms, wine production departments, and kitchens here. The abundance and the size of the rooms, halls, and living areas of the city indicate that it could shelter quite a number of people.

DERINKUYU

Derinkuyu, which was formerly called Melengübü, lies 29 kilometers to the south of Nevşehir on the Nevşehir- Niğde highway. This agrarian town is built on

the antique underground city and is therefore an attractive place for the lovers of history.

The graves surrounding the underground city point to the 7th century A.D as the time of settlement, and Derinkuyu is thought to be a little older than Kaymaklı which lies 9 kilometers away.

This underground city is estimated to have 18-20 floors and a depth of almost 40 meters carved in the soft tuff rocks of Cappadocia. Only 8 floors of this gigantic complex have been cleaned and opened up to visitors.

On the first floor right near the entrance we see a stable where the moulds for fodder are clearly identified. We see then next to the stable the rooms where grapes have been pressed and left to fermentation. After these rooms we come to a place covered with a barrel-vault which looks like a place for religious ceremonies.

There are living rooms lined on both sides of the hallway leading to the second floor. These rooms where lots of people lived together look as complicated as labyrinths. The walls of these rooms where privacy does not look

The underground city of Kaymaklı.

The underground city of Derinkuyu.

possibly have been darkened with the soot of burning fire. There are lots of cooking niches and storage moulds in the walls.

Near the kitchen we see a wine production area which is divided into a pressing room and a canal carved out of stone for the flow of grape juice. We encounter the majority of the storerooms on the third floor and there's a tunnel here that leads to the water wells. The fourth floor shelters living rooms and some more storerooms.

A long gallery stretches directly from the third floor to the fifth one and it is

constructed in such a way, that it could be closed up by a large millstone in times of danger. The ventilation pipe on the fifth floor is directly attached to the ground floor. The tunnel between the fifth and the sixth floors has living areas on both sides, and there are millstones for defence on the sixth floor as well. The moulds on the walls of the tunnels are supposed to have been for oil lamps.

The seventh floor of Derinkuyu shelters the biggest area which is supported by three pillars. We also see a well and a church with a cruciform plan here, and the speciality of this floor is a grave room at the end of a narrow tunnel. The eighth floor of Derinkuyu has a single room and a chimney for ventilation.

This underground city has approximately 52 chimneys for ventilation and a lot of cisterns and storerooms. It is estimated that 10 000 people could have found shelter in it. Derinkuyu also has a very big church with a cruciform plan, but no paintings on the walls which could have helped to determine the exact time of construction.

THE UNDERGROUND CITY OF ÖZKONAK

The underground city of Özkonak is within the city of Özkonak which lies 14 kilometers to the north of Avanos. This underground city was discovered in 1972 but the whole of it has not been brought out to daylight yet.

The part of it which is on the slope heading for the river, lies in ruins, and there are holes for communication between the floors. The big millstones for closing up the entrances of its 14 rooms do not have the usual holes at their centers.

There are holes for pouring hot oil, and for throwing arrows and spears from the labyrinths instead. It is estimated that the two big halls at the entrance have been used as stables. We can see the fire places and the casks in the kitchens and eating-rooms.

THE UNDERGROUND CITY OF ACIGÖL

The underground city of Acıgöl (bitter lake) which is on the highway between Aksaray and Nevşehir, has been cleaned and illuminated by the municipality, and is thus open to visit. This city has three entrances but only the first floor is accessible.

At this floor we see rooms, tunnels, millstones to close them up, and

ventilation openings which are common to all the underground cities of the region. Because Acıgöl is on the highway going to Nevşehir, it doesn't require much effort to visit this amazing establishment.

THE UNDERGROUND CITY OF MAZI

This city is situated near the Mazı village which is 10 kilometers to the east of Kaymaklı and which was called Mataza in antiquity.

The underground city of Mazı actually lies on the slopes of a hill to the west of the village, and is therefore not similar to the other underground cities of the region.

We also find rock graves dating back to the Roman period here. The façades of these rock graves resemble those of antique temples and one of them draws our attention with its three pillars and monumental portal.

THE UNDERGROUND CITY OF TATLARIN

This underground city is at the fortress area of the Tatlarin village which is situated 10 kilometers to the north of Acıgöl, and is accessible since 1991. Besides the edifices built in volcanic tuff, we come across quite a number of churches in the fortress area of Acıgöl.

Land erosion has devastated most of these churches whose abundance indicate that Acıgöl has been an important religious center. Because the original portal of the underground city has been ruined, we enter Tatlarin through the rooms at the western side.

Only two floors of the Tatlarin underground city are accessible today. The huge size of the rooms and the storerooms show that this place has also been used for military purposes.

AÇIKSARAY

Açıksaray is a town on the road from Nevşehir to Gülşehir, and spreads over an area of 1 square kilometers with its rock houses and stables.

It is believed to be either a monastic center, a caravanserai, a military headquarters, a big settlement, or a composition of all of these.

Because of the lack of decorated churches, the chances for it to be a monastic center decrease, and therefore we cannot estimate when it was really inhabited.

ÖRESIN HAN

This caravanserai is in the vicinity of Ağzıkarahan and was built at the end of the 13th century.

It is much smaller than the other caravanserais erected by the Seldjuk sultans and covers an area of only 520 square meters.

Its monumental portal and walls have been ruined to such an extent, that it's not possible to figure out the date of construction.

Açıksaray, a general view.

Açıksaray.

The huge natural mushroom in the vicinity of Gülşehir.

HACIBEKTAŞ

Hacıbektaş is an administrative district on the road between Nevşehir and Kırşehir to the north of the former. This agrarian town is the home town of Hacı Bektaş Veli, the founder of the Bektaşi order of Islam.

He has established his dervish convent here in the 13th century, and the town which is therefore renowned since then, is also of touristic importance today.

THE MUSEUM OF HACIBEKTAŞ

The convent and the complex of Hacıbektaş is composed of a variety of buildings situated around three courtyards extending from west to east. The convent's bath, laundry and the Üçler fountain which was built in 1897 are to be found in the first courtyard after the main portal.

The second courtyard is the principal courtyard of the convent, and an inscripted pool and the Aslanlı (lioned) fountain are situated here. At the other end of this second courtyard, we see a small soup kitchen and a mosque erected by Sultan Mahmud II.

The cooking pots and other kitchen utensils are on display in the soup kitchen now. The guest house and the storeroom are at the left side of the courtyard. The inscript of the central house tells us that it was built in 1367, and this is the most important section of the complex because it is the locality where the admittance ceremony and the religious congragations were held.

We see the throne of the Bektaşi order, the rank costumes, and the pictures relating to the order in this section now. The third courtyard shelters the tombs of the order superiors as well as the mausoleum of the founder of the Bektaşi order, Hacı Bektaş Veli. The dome of this mausoleum is decorated with floral patterns and scripts.

A view from the dreamland of Göreme.

The museum of Hacı Bektaş Veli.

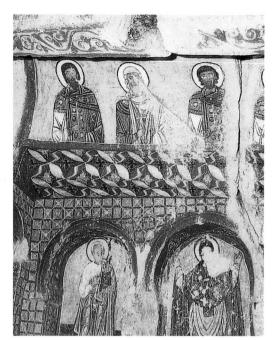

G Ö R E M E
Matiana-Maçan-Avcılar

Göreme was called Maçan in antiquity and is one of the oldest sites in this region. The oldest known source where the name of this city is mentioned, is the book titled " The Doings of St. Hieron" of the 7th century.

Maçan was not a city naturally protected and hidden from the eye, therefore it suffered a lot from the Arab raids and lost the majority of its population. The churches of Maçan were rebuilt after the Arab invasions were over. It is generally accepted that the city was situated by the side of a river in its earliest times, and there are indeed two pillared mausoleums left from this early stage as proof of this early settlement. There are five churches in the village of Göreme and its surroundings. The biggest of these is the Durmuş Kadir Church which is thought to have been built in either the 6th or the 7th century. Its pillars and the preacher's desk are well preserved. The other churches of Göreme have been built in the 10th and the 11th centuries after the Arab raids. The youngest church here is the Yusuf Koç Church which was built in the 11th century when Göreme had an episcopate. Two of the churches of Göreme, the Bezirhanı Church and the Orta Mahalli Church are within the city, and the farthest church which can be reached in 30 minutes on foot, is the Church of Karabulut dating back to the 11th century.

The most attractive settlement of the region is the village of Göreme which is an unsurpassed example of the harmony of man and nature. People still live in the rock houses or use them as storerooms today, displaying an immense reverence for this volcanic earth and history. The village of Göreme does not only have rock houses, but also rock restaurants and rock hotels which all visitors find amazing. The natural boundaries of the city are drawn by the high rocks

Views from the valley of Göreme.

The Church of El Nazar.

surrounding it and the fairy chimneys within; it's a place that offers unbelievable natural treasures.

EL NAZAR

The Church of El Nazar is carved out of a rock which looks like a tent and is one of the most interesting buildings of the Göreme region. The side walls of this church, which was built in the 10th century, have collapsed. The paintings of this church, which is very harmonious with the natural formations in its surroundings, are well preserved in spite of the time and erosion of hundreds of years. We see very stylish figures on the walls of this church. There's the figure of Christ ascending to the heavens on a rainbow in the central dome. On the western arch we see the scenes of the annunciation, the visit, the introduction to the temple; and on the southern arch

p. 56-57: Supernatural views from the valley of Göreme.

there are the scenes of the birth of Christ, the epiphany, and the escape to Egypt. Scenes showing the ablution of Christ and the pursuit of Elizabeth are to be found on the western wall. Besides these themes, we also see the descent into hell, the crucifixion, the baptism, and the transformation of Christ in this church. Furthermore the Church of El Nazar has the pictures of emperor Constantine and his mother Helen.

THE VALLEY OF GÖRKÜNDERE

The valley of Görkündere can be reached by a narrow foothpath which lies between the village of Görkündere and the Görkündere Open Air Museum. It's a valley worth seeing with its high fairy chimneys and wonderful rock formations. This valley cannot be reached by car, and its unique vineyards and sunflower fields among the huge rocks leave everyone breathless.

THE VALLEY OF
KILIÇLAR

This valley is between the valleys of Aktepe (the white hill) and Göreme. The valley of Kılıçlar is one of the most beautiful valleys of Cappadocia but because it can only be reached on foot, it isn't visited frequently.

Kılıçlar has a lot of churches, the most famous of which is the Kılıçlar Church, and this valley is just cut out for photography fans.

The Kılıçlar Church is called " the mirrored Church" in vernacular. It has a plan in the form of a closed Greek cross, rests on four pillars, and is dated back to the 10th century.

In the central dome we see the ascension of Christ, and on the pendentives of the dome the figures of the four Gospel writers.

There are more biblical scenes on the arches encircling the dome, and the figures of the Saints and the Cappadocian clergymen. The Kılıçlar Church is significant with its size and pictures among all the churches built in the 10th century.

Panaromic views from Göreme.

THE OPEN AIR MUSEUM OF GÖREME

A panoramic view from the vicinity of Göreme.

The Open Air Museum of Göreme.

Göreme is taken under protection as an open air museum today. Its rock churches refrectories and houses indicate that Göreme has been a large monastic settlement since the ninth century.

The abundance of religious buildings is an indicator of Göreme's importance as a monastic center rather than an agricultural settlement.

Only one of Göreme's churches dates back to the 6th-7th century, and the rest have been built in the second half of the 9th century when the city started to flourish.

The majority of Göreme's churches are small with a single room but two of them differ noticeably from the rest. These are the Kılıçlar Church and the two Tokalı churches built in the tenth century, and which have some remarkable examples of Byzantine pictoral art.

We encounter "the golden period" of

Byzantine art in " the pillared churches" of the 11th century when the churches were decorated with fabulous paintings. The churches of the 11th century differ from the rest in the choice of religious themes and architecture, and they represent the so-called aristocratic art of the 11th century.

The themes of their paintings, their iconography, and the details of floral decorations are the same and therefore create the impression, that this repetition has come out of the same artists' studio. The human figures are delicately made, and they usually wear wet-looking garments that display their bodily structure.

The faces have a sad and affectionate expression. Furthermore the distribution of the religious pictures over the walls and arches is perfect.

Since the Göreme, Kılıçlar and El Nazar valleys shelter quite a number of churches, it may not be easy to visit them in a few days. Though we can't estimate when monastic life has ended in these valleys, we know that only a few churches have been built after the 11th century.

The bedrooms, benches, tables, and storerooms carved out of the rocks in the vicinity of these churches show that small monastic units have existed here.

We also see some names inscribed on the paintings in the 18th and 19th centuries, and this fact indicates that the churches of Göreme have been visited for pilgrimage, and that the pilgrims have carved their own names on the walls.

Three different views from Göreme Open Air Museum.

THE GIRLS' MONASTERY

The Open Air Museum of Göreme, the Girls' Monastery.

The big rock massif right at the entrance of the Göreme Open Air Museum is called the Girls' Monastery. The churches, refrectories and tunnels in the four floors of this rock show that this place has been a monastery. A metal staircase leads us to a well-preserved eating- room which has a nice table carved out of rocks.

We see the remnants of four churches in this rock massif, and in the one near the eating-room, which has three apsides and a barrel-vault, the scenes of the birth of Christ are very well-made. Furthermore we see scenes from Cappadocia's St.

Georgius' life and his martyrdom on the southern wall of this church.

The second church of this rock massif is the Girls' Church from which it acquired its name. The Girls' Church has a Greek cross plan and its central dome rests upon four pillars. The sole picture of the church shows Jesus Christ standing.

THE ELMALI CHURCH (THE APPLE CHURCH)

The Elmalı Church has four pillars and three apsides. The original entrance at the southern side is not used today. The religious scenes are distributed very evenly among the arches, the domes, and the walls. We see the Deisis (Virgin Mary, Jesus Christ and St. John the Baptist) on the central apsis.

The figure of Jesus Christ at the central dome, which is supported by four thin columns, is surrounded by pendentives with the figures of the four Gospel writers on them. We find the pictures of the archangels at the smaller domes towards the apsis and the ascension of Christ at the southern cupola.

The distribution of scenes:

The left apsis: Virgin Mary and Jesus Christ

Over the left apsis: The Burial of Christ

The central apsis: Virgin Mary, Jesus Christ and St. John the Baptist

The right apsis: Archangel Michael

Over the right apsis: The last supper

The northern wall: The birth of Christ and the arrival in Jerusalem

The western wall: The resurrection of Lazarus, Virgin Mary and the Apostles and Baptism

The southern wall: The transformation of Christ, the Crucifixion and the descent into Hell

The Appled Church, the fresco of Jesus the Saviour at the lateral dome.

The Appled Church, the fresco of Jesus the Saviour at the central dome.

THE ST. BARBARA CHURCH

The Barbara Church is the most disputable church of the region because of its frescoes. The central dome of this church is supported by two columns and corner walls. Its plan looks like that of the Çarıklı Church with the side entrance and the three apsides. Though very much devastated, the pediment at the entrance can still be noticed. We see the figure of a sitting and consecrating Christ at the central apsis.

The two famous saints of Cappadocia, Georgius and Theodorus, are pictured killing the dragon on the northern wall which faces the entrance. The figure of St. Barbara who gives the name of the church, is to be found on the western wall. Furthermore Falibon and Leon whose names appear on the inscripts, are thought to be the erecters of the church.

Researchers and travellers have been discussing the pictures of the Barbara Church since a long time because the meanings of these are quite obscure. Next to the stylized cedar trees and the rooster which symbolizes alertness and the betrayal of St. Petrus, we see the picture of a grasshopper on the northern wall. The grasshopper moving towards the cross symbolizes the christening of various peoples.

We see a lot of crosses and mysterious symbols painted all over the church. These red diagrammatic forms like crosses, triangles, columns, medals, and unidentified animals were probably painted by the first rock carvers to protect themselves from ill omens.

There are also interpreters who think that the Barbara Church dates back to the Iconoclastic Period precisely because of these mysterious figures.

The St. Barbara Church.

THE SERPENT CHURCH

The plan of this rectangular church, which is covered by a barrel-vault, is not regular like those of the other churches. There's a grave room at its southern end. The pictures of the Serpent Church do not follow up a sequence, but are painted as seperate panels.

The name of this church comes from the dragon which was killed by the famous Cappadocian saints, Georgius and Theodorus, and this scene is to be found at the left of the entrance.

Following this picture, we come to the portraits of Emperor Constantine and his mother Helen, who was the discoverer of the original cross of the crucifixion in the Holy Land. Constantine was the first

The Serpent Church, St. Georgius and St. Theodor fighting the dragon.

Roman emperor to convert to Christianity, and there are lots of legends and happenings in their lives concerning the cross. This emperor and his mother appear often in the church paintings of Cappadocia.

Facing this picture, we find the frescoes of St. Onuphrius, St. Thomas and St. Basilius. According to the legend, St. Onophrius was a clergyman who had lived sixty years long at the Egyptian desert.

St. Onophrius went into the local legends because of his stylized chest muscles, and it is believed that he was originally a woman who was transformed into a man when he wanted to dedicate his life to Christianity.

THE ESKI TOKALI CHURCH

This church is the grandest of all churches in Cappadocia, and is actually composed of two churches built at different times. The first one of these is the Eski Tokalı which was built in the beginning of the 10th century and which is covered by a barrel-vault. This church is classified as an "archaic church" because of its paintings that follow one another like a film strip. It's assumed that its paintings have been done by an artists' studio which has painted other churches in the region as well. We distinguish pre-byzantine, byzantine and eastern influences in the paintings. The hand, arm and body movements of the stylized figures fit in a certain scheme.

The distribution of scenes:

The southern side of the barrel-vault (at the right of the entrance):

The scenes at the very top: The annunciation, the visit of Elizabeth, the journey to Betlehem, the birth of Christ, and the scene where Jesus turns water to wine

The middle section: The pursuit of Elizabeth and John the child, themes concerning St. John the Baptist, and the wedding at Canaan

The scenes below: The last supper, the judgement of Pilatus, and the road to Golgatha (Calvary)

The northern side of the barrel-vault: The three kings worshipping, the massacre of children, the escape to Egypt, and the murder of Zachariah

The middle section: Jesus turns water to wine, the vocation of the apostles, the increase of bread, the healing of the blind man, and the resurraction of Lazarus

The scenes below: The crucifixion, Jesus being taken from the crucifix, the

A view of the frescoes of the Tokalı Church.

burial, the women at the grave, the descent into Hell, and the ascension of Christ

THE YENI TOKALI CHURCH

The Eski and Yeni Tokalı churches form the shape of a T together. The distribution of the religious scenes over the barrel-vaults, the arches, and the walls in the Yeni Tokalı Church reflect a wonderful harmony. This second church has a " transverse plan" where the apsides are placed at the longer wall. The transverse plan which was first applied in Mesopotamia was adopted by the Anatolians later on. The Yeni Tokalı Church was built in 950-960 A.D. and is an expression of the golden age of the " Macedonian Renaissance" in the Byzantine Empire. An inscript on the

northern apsis informs us that the painter of the church was Nicephoros and its builders were Constantine and Leon.

The colors and the style of the pictures are clearly different from those of the Eski Tokalı Church. The figures here are elongated, more beautiful, and more eloquent. The ground color of this church is an extraordinary navy blue and though the themes of the pictures resemble those of the first church, they are drawn more elegantly.

The distribution of scenes:

The left apsis: Jesus and the angels, Mary of Egypt, and the hospitality of Abraham

The main apsis: The crucifixion, Jesus being carried away from the crucifix, the burial of Christ, and the descent into Hell

The scenes on the barrel-vault:

The middle section (on the eastern side): The ascension of Christ surrounded by Virgin Mary and the apostles. (On the

western side): The benediction of the apostles.

(On the southern side): Pentecost. On this picture, the apostles have lined up in two rows, and the crowds behind the kings are listening to the sermon.

(On the southeastern side): The appointment of seven new priests

(On the southwestern side): The apostles leaving Jerusalem to go to distant lands

(On the northeastern side): The visit, the annunciation, and Jesus turning water to wine

(On the northwestern side): The birth of Christ, and the three kings

The northern frieze: Jesus and St. John the Baptist, Satan trying to mislead Jesus, and Jesus summoning his first apostles

The eastern frieze: The healing of the blind man, the healing of the leper, the healing of the widow's child, and the healing of the man with a crippled arm

The southern frieze: The healing of Jairus' daughter, the healing of the paralyzed, the arrival in Jerusalem, and the last supper

THE DARK CHURCH

The Dark Church and convent complex is the most famous establishment among the pillared churches of the Göreme Open Air Museum. It is composed of a series of buildings around a small courtyard. The buildings carved in the rocks lying to the south of the courtyard have two floors. Most of the researchers think that the Dark Church was the first of the pillared churches. They also maintain that the Elmalı and the Çarıklı churches have been built by the same persons. The paintings of the Dark Church have been very well preserved because very little daylight can ooze into this building. Its plan is that of a closed Greek cross with four columns and six cupolas. There are a grave room and a rectangular narthex covered by a barrel-vault at the entrance. At the narthex, we see the ascension of

Views from the frescoes of the Dark Church.

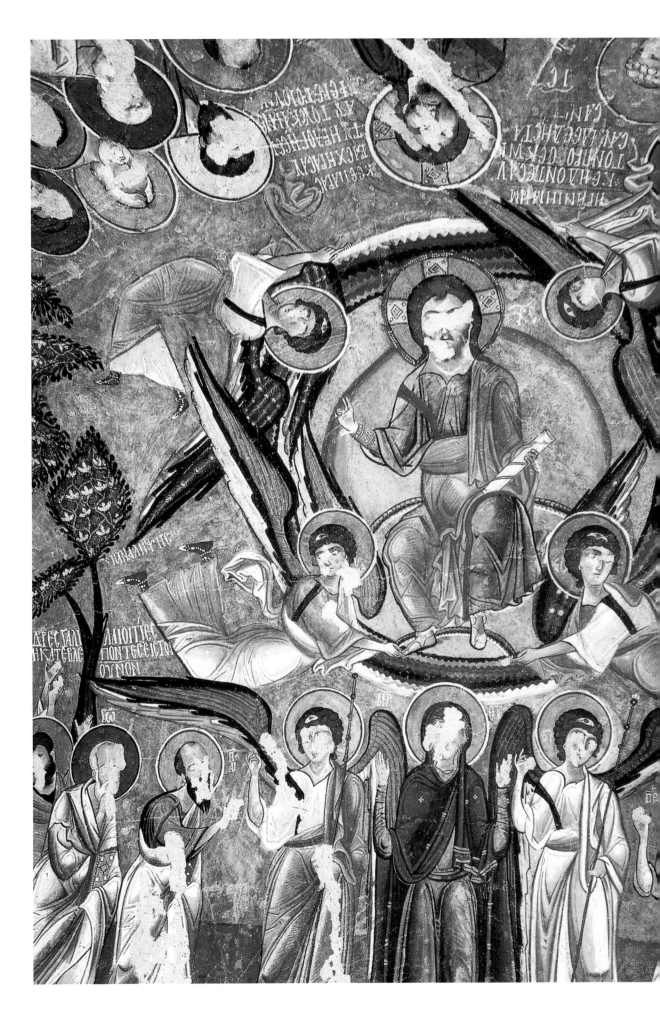

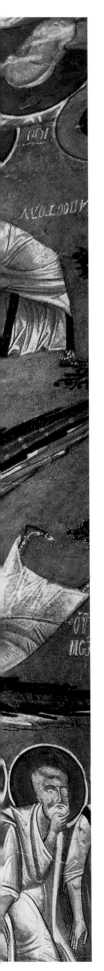

Christ and the praying apostles. Jesus is seated on a double rainbow here carried by four angel figures.

The distribution of scenes:

The central apsis: Virgin Mary, Jesus Christ and St. John the Baptist

The northern apsis: Virgin Mary

The central dome: Jesus Christ, the angels in medals and the saints on pendentives

The southern barrel-vault: The betrayal of Jehovah

The northern barrel-vault: The birth of Christ, the adoration of the three kings

The western barrel-vault: The arrival in Jerusalem

The western wall: The resurrection of Lazarus, the transformation of Christ and Baptism

The northern wall: The journey to Betlehem, the birth of Christ, Matthew and St. John

The southern wall: The women at the grave, the Crucifixion and the three Jews thrown into fire

The eastern wall: The last supper, Lucas and Matthew.

THE ÇARIKLI CHURCH
(THE CHURCH WITH THE SANDAL)

This church is situated on the peak of the biggest rock of the Göreme Open Air Museum and is to be reached by metal stairs today. The partly ruined religious paintings of the church are still in a fairly good state. The eating-room right below the church shows that this place has been a monastic complex like the other ones. The picture of " The Last Supper" behind the rock table of the eating-room has been very well preserved. The plan of the church is that of a closed Greek cross, and the central dome is supported by two columns at the east and by corner walls at the west. It is believed that the interesting name of the church (the shod church) comes from the footprint on the floor, and that this church was built because of it. The catchiest details of this

Views from the frescoes of the Dark Church.

Çavuşin Village.

church appear on the western wall. Among these, we can name the scene showing the four builders of the church and the inscript where the words, " the holy cross" are carved. A figure with a turban on his head is not less important either.

The distribution of scenes:

The central apsis: Virgin Mary, Jesus Christ and St. John the Baptist

The northern apsis: Mary and Jesus

Over the northern apsis: The hospitality of Abraham

The southern apsis: The figure of Gabriel

The central dome: Jesus and the angels in medals

THE HIDDEN CHURCH

This church which was discovered in 1957, has acquired this name because it's quite difficult to reach it. It was built in the 11th century and is situated on the slope between the Göreme and El Nazar valleys.

It has a " transverse plan" like the Tokalı Church and has two pillars.

One of the well-preserved pictures of this church shows Veronica's face cover. Its speciality is the big and very ornate cross which covers the dome and is actually seen in early churches.

ÇAVUŞIN

The old Çavuşin village which was deserted because of the falling rocks, is one of the most interesting settlements of Cappadocia. The houses of Çavuşin which all have lovely façade decorations, are the silent witnesses of the past glamour of this settlement.

THE CHURCH OF ST. JOHN THE BAPTIST

This church is situated at the top of the Çavuşin fortress and its double-columned façade could be seen from everywhere once. It's one of the oldest churches of this region and has unique pictures, which we see only in the earlier churches. It is believed to have been built in the 5th century and is damaged to a great extent today. We see the scenes of the decapitation of St. John the Baptist, the dance of Salome, and the feast of Herod here. This is also the church where the hand of St. Jerome is kept. St. Jerome was born in Cappadocia and was killed in Malatya in the era of Emperor Diocletianus. This church was so important in the Byzantine era, that St. Jerome's holy belongings were kept here, and it was elaborately decorated.

BÜYÜK GÜVERCİNLİK (THE BIG DOVECOT)

The second important church of Çavuşin is the" Büyük Güvercinlik" which was built for and dedicated to the Byzantine emperor Nicephorus Phocas. It was built during the " Macedonian Renaissance" and has a single hall with a cradle-vault. It has been built in memory of the visit of Nicephorus Phocas and is therefore very important. We can see the emperor with his family in a painting on the northern apsis.

The village of Çavuşin, general view.

GÜLLÜDERE AND KIZILÇUKUR

A walkway starting from Çavuşin brings us to two wonderful valleys of Cappadocia. The early churches and the rock formations among the trees and the fields take us to a world of mystery we have yet to discover. Güllüdere is one of these valleys where we find five churches. One of these churches has an inscript which reads the name of emperor Constantine Porphyrogenetus and can therefore be dated. The other churches of Güllüdere have been built in the 7th-10th centuries. The valley of Kızılçukur is also worth a visit especially because of the well-preserved Church of St. Anne and the Cross Church at the opposite end of the valley, where people have sought refuge during the Arab raids.

The village of Çavuşin.

A view of the valley of Kızılçukur.

Çavuşin, the Church of Büyük Güvercinlik.
The outer view and some of its frescoes.

p. 78-79: Tree views from the valley of Kızılvadi.

PAŞABAĞ

The formation of Cappadocia's fairy chimneys can best be observed in the valley of Paşabağı which is in the vicinity of Zelve.

The fairy chimneys of Paşabağı with their two or three "hats" exhibit an unsurpassed view and rise today among the vineyards and sunflower fields.

They have been the settlements of ascetic monks in the Byzantine era. In one of these fairy chimneys we come across the scenes taken from the life of St. Simeon, who is said to have lived on top of a pillar in the Byzantine period, and had a far-reaching fame.

Paşabağ.

Mysterious natural views from Paşabağ.

THE OPEN AIR MUSEUM OF ZELVE

Zelve is a settlement carved in the rocks, and shows how perfectly man can adapt himself to nature. The road from Paşabağı leads us through the reddish terrain of volcanic earth and takes us to Zelve, which is protected as an open air museum today.

Three natural valleys formed by erosions and rock subsidences, and surrounded by steep rocks and thousands of rock houses, churches, and tunnels carved in them, create an unforgettable impression on the visitors. The inhabitants who have brilliantly carved the volcanic earth to be protected from cold in winter and heat in summer, have erected houses, churches, convents, and pigeon houses in this manner for hundreds of years.

The churches of Zelve, the paintings of which have been quite devastated through time, have been built during the the Iconoclastic Period and before. The majority of these churches are decorated with symbols like the cross, the fish, the grapes, and the deer, befitting the tradition of the early Byzantine iconography.

There are no churches in Zelve which are confined to religious paintings, and thus we can conclude that the inhabitants of Zelve have been against church painting even before the Iconoclastic Crisis of the 8th century. The few painted churches that we see have been erected after the Iconoclastic Crisis.

We cannot reach the first valley of Zelve directly because of rock subsidences, but a road starting at the second valley takes us to the first one, which is of an amazing size and magnificence. On this road we see the Geyikli Church (the Deered Church) where a huge cross and deer pictures attract our attention.

The rock houses of Zelve have been occupied until recent times, and a mosque carved in the rocks of the first

Entrance to Zelve Valley.

valley and architectural additions made of cement are an evidence of a long past. A speciality of Zelve which attracts our attention is the presence of the innumerate dovecotes, specifically seen in the first valley.

Pigeons have played an important role in the lives of the inhabitants who have fed on their flesh and used their dung. And the designs which have been carefully and delicately put around the pigeon holes are so various, that they can be the theme of a seperate observation.

In the third valley which is not often visited, we find the Church of Grapes which has two halls and was built before the Iconoclastic Period, and the Cross Church which was built during it.

Views from the Open Air Museum of Zelve and its surroundings.

THE VALLEY OF
DERBENT

This valley is situated between Avanos, Zelve, and Ürgüp, and is called "the pink valley" because of the color of its soil. The new road that cuts the valley enables the visitors to reach its beauties. This valley is called "Devrent" in vernacular, and is very appropriate for examining rock formations and the fairy chimneys. This valley has never been inhabited and we see neither houses nor churches here. The visitors should leave the main road and climb the slopes to enjoy the fairy chimneys with different shapes.

The valley of Zelve.

Views from the valley of Derbent.

A V A N O S

Avanos was called Venessa in antiquity and was an important settlement. It is estimated that the city's name comes from " Venessa" which was the Roman name for it. Remnants of the Old Hittite and Mid-Hittite periods have been discovered in the excavations made in Topaklı Höyük near Avanos. Since the traces of a local Zeus cult and hellenistic mausoleums have also been found, we can conclude that Avanos has been an important settlement in other epochs as well.

The city was ruled by the Seldjuk Turks after the Byzantine era, and after the Seldjuks it became a part of the Ottoman Empire in 1466. Avanos has two mosques left from the Seldjuk and Ottoman periods.

The former one is the Alaeddin Mosque and the Ottoman one is the Yeraltı (Underground) Mosque, which has no inscript but is dated back to the 16th century.

Avanos is divided into two by the Kızılırmak river which is the longest river of Anatolia. It is renowned with pottery and carpet making.

The art of pottery making goes back to the times of the Hittites and is very developed in the Avanos area. The local population uses the earth taken from the shores of Kızılırmak, mixes it with sand and clay, and creates the muddy substance for pottery.

Technological development which led to the use of mechanical refrigeration since the 60ies, and the installment of pipelines for the distribution of water caused the decline of pottery's importance. But it is still a source of income as a handicraft.

Avanos, a settlement in Cappadocia, famous for pottery and tile-works.

The potter's statue decorating the center of Avanos.

Avanos, ladies weaving carpets.

Handmade Turkish carpets displayed in modern carpet centers attract admiration of many visitors in Cappadocia.

U Ç H I S A R

The peak of the natural formations of Cappadocia is without any doubt the Fortress of Uçhisar.

We recommend this sight to all the lovers of natural wonders fervently. What the inhabitants call "Fortress" is actually two gigantic rocks which are surrounded by smaller rocks that look like towers. These amazing geological formations of Cappadocia which we can call "the fortress cities", and where the inhabitants have sought security have two outstanding examples, namely that of Uçhisar and Ortahisar.

The rock massif of Uçhisar was inhabited in both the Byzantine and the Ottoman periods, and we can see the traces of these settlements even today. People have lived in the Uçhisar fortress and its outskirts till recent times but have left the area because of rock erosion.

Uçhisar which offers the most beautiful rock formations, wonderful valleys, and an extraordinary castle surprises and moves all onlookers.

Incredible views from Uçhisar.

p.92-93: Nature in the environment of Uçhisar.

ORTAHISAR

Ortahisar has been erected around a big rock massif which rises in the shape of a castle. Even the peak of this castle can be reached which was originally built for military and civil purposes. The view of the city and the circumscribing valleys from the highest point of Uçhisar is really unmatched.

We advise the panorama lovers to walk towards the river, go over the stone bridge, and climb the slope facing it. The view of Ortahisar from this point with all the traditional stone houses clustered around the rock massif will startle everyone. The churches and the convents in the valley near the city are the evidences of the cultural past of the city.

THE CANBAZLI CHURCH

This is one of the rare churches priest Jerphanion has not discovered. It is also known as the "Aşağı Bağ Church".

This church is situated at the lower skirts of the Ortahisar castle and is opened to visits only lately. It has the plan of a closed Greek cross. Although the paintings in this church resemble the one of the churches of Göreme, it's not easy to estimate the date of erection.

THE HALLAÇ MONASTERY

This monastery is situated to the northeast of Ortahisar. It's composed of various buildings encircling a courtyard. In the church of the complex which is dedicated to Basilius the Great, there are fresco paintings from the 10th and 11th centuries. The grave room and the kitchen are obvious and in another room, there is a human figure with open arms.

THE CHURCHES OF THE BALKAN STREAM

The Balkan stream lies two kilometers away from Ortahisar, and can be reached either on foot or with a donkey ride. The churches of the Balkan stream are dated back to the Iconoclastic Period as well as the Archaic Period. They are important because both of these periods display early Byzantine art.

Views from Ortahisar and its environment.

Ü R G Ü P

Ürgüp was called " Assiana" in antiquity and has been an important settlement throughout the ages. It acquired the name " Başhisar" (Chief Castle) in the Seldjuk period and lies 18 kilometers away from Nevşehir.

It's one of the pretty cities of the region with its splendid castle right in the middle of the city, and its Turkish architecture. Besides its rock houses carved in the mountains during the Byzantine and Ottoman periods, Ürgüp's stone houses with their ornate façades are also very attractive. We can see the most beautiful houses of the region in Ürgüp indeed.

We can mention the Kadı Castle, the Karamanoğulları Mosque, the Altıkapı Mausoleum, and the Tahsinağa Library among the monuments of the Turkish period. Ürgüp's hotels, touristic establishments, and shops are the main sources of income.

Ürgüp, general view.

Fairy chimneys, the symbols of Cappadocia near Ürgüp.

MUSTAFAPAŞA

Mustafapaşa is a settlement that's 6 kilometers away from Ürgüp. Its churches of the late Byzantine period, houses decorated with animal figures and various designs, caravanserai built in the Ottoman period, and stone houses and rock churches make it a center of attraction. The cultural heritage of the city shows immediately that Mustafapaşa has been one of the most important towns in the Byzantine and Ottoman periods.

One of the churches here has been built in the 19th century, and is Cappadocia's latest rock church which makes it very special.

Two typical views from Cappadocia.

Mustafapaşa, view from the Monastery of Hagios Vasilios.

Street scene from Mustafapaşa.

THE SOĞANLI VALLEY

This valley lies 34 kilometers away from Ürgüp and is famous with its natural beauty as well as its churches. The pigeon houses of Soğanlı, the church frescoes made by the best artists of the times, the rocks chiseled in the form of churches, and an unmatched nature are a few of the reasons why you should visit this valley.

People have dwelt in this valley since early Christianity, but the churches date back to the 9th-13th centuries. The exact dates of construction of some of these churches are known, and therefore helpful for estimating the construction dates of the other churches of

The village of Soğanlı.

Cappadocia. The churches of Soğanlı have a rather different architecture and a different iconography. They are therefore of a special importance among the other churches of the region.

Especially the " domed churches" where the rocks have been chiseled from the outside in order to imitate the churches made of stone, are unique in all Cappadocia. The paintings of such churches, where the cupolas and their drums are noticeable from the outside, have been partially preserved.

THE CANAVAR CHURCH

Like many churches of the region, this church is also called after the dragon killed by St. Georgius, and is one of the most beautiful churches of Cappadocia.

Its frescoes are dated back to the 11th and the 13th centuries. On the apsis we see a figure of Christ surrounded by Virgin Mary and St. John the Baptist. We also see a painting where Jesus distributes bread and wine to his apostles. The scene of the "Last Judgement" on the barrel-vault which covers the main hall is very detailed and well-done.

THE CHURCH OF KARABAŞ (DARK HEAD)

This church was built in 1060/61. A long inscript informs us that it was erected at the time of the Byzantine emperor Constantine Dukas, and that the best artists of the time were hired to decorate it. This church, which was built on the eve of the arrival of the Seldjuk Turks in Anatolia, has been painted by the most talented artist or artists of the age.

The most important scene of the church is the painting where Christ distributes bread and wine to his apostles, which is inside a deep niche. Beside this painting, we also find the scenes of the birth, the introduction to the temple, the crucifixion, and the descent into hell here in this church.

THE DOMED CHURCHES

These three churches, which are made by chiselling the conic rocks in imitaton of churches made of stone, are unforgettable for all visitors. They have pointed cupolas and high drums, and

their paintings have been done mainly in the 10th century.

The most important of these churches is the Hidden Church where the pictures are quite devastated, but still maintain the scenes concerning St. Peter and St. Paul. The pictures showing these saints with emperor Nero, and the torture of St. Peter and St. Paul are rarely seen in Cappadocia, and are therefore important.

THE BARBARA CHURCH

The inscript of the church tells us that it was built in the first quarter of the 11th century.

The patron saint of the church was Basileus, who is thought to have been a commander on duty in this region. The researchers believe that this church is a product of the transitional phase between the " archaic churches" where the pictures have been organized like a film strip, and the " pillared churches" of Cappadocia.

We see here the scenes of the seven sleepers of Ephesus, the birth of Christ, the test of water, and the descent into hell.

KAYSERI

Kayseri is established by the side of the plain which is watered by Karasu (the dark stream) at the northern outskirts of Mount Erciyes.

It is a lively commercial center well-known for textile, sugar, and airplane repair industries today. Kayseri has been inhabited since early history and we see the evidences of this long history in the finds of the Kültepe and Eğriköy excavations.

Following the Early Bronze Age, the Period of the Assyrian Trade Colonies, and the Hittite Period, Kayseri and its surroundings were called the Tabal Land in the Late Hittite Period.

It was first ruled by the Assyrians and then by the Medes, and became the center of the Cappadocian Strapy in 550 A.D under the rule of the Persians. It was called "Mazaka" at this age. Kayseri went under Macedonian rule after the visit of Alexander the Great.

After his death, the Persian Ariarathes dynasty became the ruler of the independent Kingdom of Cappadocia with its capital at Kayseri.

The city was called " Eusebeia" during the rule of this dynasty. The Ariarathes dynasty ruled this region until 90 B.C when the King of Pontus, Mithridates, assigned his own son to the Cappadocian throne.

The Romans took hold of Cappadocia again in 66 B.C. Kayseri remained under Byzantian rule for hundreds of years and was faced with frequent Arabic invasions. After the war of Manzikert (1071), it became an important center of the Seldjuk Empire, but was conquered by the Crusaders in 1097.

The city was then ruled by the Danişmendoğulları which was another Turkish principality, the Seldjuks, and the Mongols after the war of Kösedağ (1243) consecutively.

Kayseri went through a number of wars till it was finally conquered by the Ottomans in 1515.

THE FORTRESS OF KAYSERI

According to geographer Strabon, Caesarea (hence the modern name Kayseri) had no town walls in antiquity. It is estimated that the first town walls have been built against probable invasions coming from the east. The sources of the 6th century A.D inform us that these walls were erected under the Byzantine Emperor Justinianus.

The town walls have been fortified and enlarged in the Seldjuk, Karamanoğlu, and Ottoman periods consecutively, and therefore have been altered to a great extent. The fortress of Kayseri is composed of inner and outer citadels today, and is one of the most beautiful examples of Turkish military architecture.

ULU CAMI
(THE GRAND MOSQUE)

An inscript tells us that the Grand Mosque of Kayseri was built in 1135-1150. It used to be the biggest mosque in Kayseri of the times with its area of 1750 square meters.

It has eight squares built parallel to the prayer niche and two domes. A school and the rooms of the students are built beside the mosque.

THE HUAND HATUN COMPLEX

This complex which is composed of a mosque, a school, a bath, and a mausoleum is one of the first and most beautiful group of buildings in Anatolia. It was erected by the Seldjuk Sultan Alaeddin Keykubad's mother Mahperi Hatun in 1238.

THE KURŞUNLU MOSQUE
(THE LEADEN MOSQUE)

This small mosque is thought to have been constructed by the famous architect Sinan in 1584.

Its dome is covered with lead on the outside and therefore the name. Though it's small, it's one of the most famous monuments of Kayseri.

Kayseri, general view.

Kayseri is a Turkish city famous for its carpets.

THE REVOLVING DOME
(DÖNER KÜMBET)

Kayseri is known as the city of mausoleums, the most famous of which is the Revolving Dome lying to the southwest of the city. It was built in 1276 for Sultan Alaeddin Keykubad's daughter Cihan Hatun. It's one of the masterpieces of the Seldjuk art of stone-cutting with plant and animal figures, and geometric designs on it.

THE ŞİFAIYE MEDRESESİ
(THE SCHOOL OF REMEDY)

Another Sultan of the Seldjuk Empire, Gıyaseddin Keyhüsrev, ordered this school to be built in 1202-1206. It is the oldest school of medicine and its hospital of the Seldjuk period in Anatolia.

THE ARCHAEOLOGICAL MUSEUM

This museum shelters the most selected monuments of all Anatolian civilizations. Consequently it's useful for the comprehension of Anatolia's long and complex history.

This museum which was opened in 1969, is one of the most significant regional museums of central Anatolia. In its garden we see a copy of the Fractin monument, the original of which is in southern Kayseri.

Another important Hittite memorial of this museum is the lions of Göllüdağ. In the glass windows of the museum we find the famous Cappadocian tablets, the statues of the Anatolian mother goddesses, examples of Hittite pottery, the beautiful İmamkulu fresco which shows the Hittite god of storm, and innumerate monuments from the Hellenistic and Roman periods.

Kayseri, the Revolving Dome.

Sultansazlığı is a beautiful aviary.

SULTAN SAZLIĞI

This is an aviary near Kayseri which houses 251 species of birds. It is one of the best bird paradises of the world, and 20 of the 72 species that are on the point of extinction, incubate here. It is also a rare place where cranes, herons, flamingos, and pelicans incubate together. All of these birds can be observed and enjoyed after February.

NIĞDE

Niğde has been founded on the outskirts of a fortress, and is full of mosques, schools and mausoleums left from the Seldjuk and the Ottoman ages. Though the city has a very long history, it emerged as an important town as late as the 12th century. Niğde was called either "Nahita" or "Nikita" in the age of the Hittites. It acquired the name Nikde in the Ottoman era, and became Niğde after the Turkish Republic was founded (1923).

The Seldjuk Sultan Alaeddin Keykubad restored and revived Niğde, and so the city became an important center of culture and trade. But the Arab geographer Ibni Batuta who visited Niğde in 1333, wrote that the city was ruined very much as a result of the wars between the Karamanoğlu dynasty and the Mongols. In the following years the

Niğde, the Ulu Mosque.

Niğde, the Eski Gümüş Monastery.

city's rulers changed continuously until 1470, when it joined the Ottoman Empire during the rule of the Conqueror Sultan Mehmed II. Niğde's Seldjuk and Ottoman monuments are relatively well-preserved.

ESKI GÜMÜŞ (THE OLD SILVER)

This is a rock church in the village of Gümüşler which lies on the northeast of Niğde. We can reach the church over a road that leads eastwards from the fifth kilometer of the highway between Niğde and Kayseri.

We enter the courtyard of the monastery through a long corridor. This courtyard is encircled by a number of rooms of the monastery. Its frescoes of the pre-Byzantine age and the non-religious scenes in the church (like the scenes of hunt) indicate that it has a very

far-reaching history.

The restoration of this complex has shown that the frescoes were painted by three different artists at different times. The frescoes date back to the 11th and the 12th centuries, and Eski Gümüş is one of the biggest convents of the region.

CAPPADOCIA

C O N T E N T S